American Revolution
Reference Library
Cumulative Index

American Revolution
Reference Library
Cumulative Index

Cumulates Indexes For:

American Revolution: Almanac
American Revolution: Biographies
American Revolution: Primary Sources

Lawrence W. Baker,
Index Coordinator

AN IMPRINT OF THE GALE GROUP

DETROIT · SAN FRANCISCO · LONDON
BOSTON · WOODBRIDGE, CT

American Revolution Reference Library Cumulative Index

Lawrence W. Baker, *Index Coordinator*

Copyright © 2000
U•X•L, an imprint of The Gale Group
27500 Drake Road
Farmomgton Hills, MI 48331-3535

Cover illustrations of Crispus Attucks and George Washington, courtesy of the Library of Congress; King George III, reproduced by permission of The Granger Collection, Ltd.; and Paul Revere's ride, reproduced by permission of Archive Photos.

Printed in the United States of America

10 9 8 7 6 5 4 3 2 1

American Revolution Reference Library Cumulative Index

A = American Revolution: Almanac
B = American Revolution: Biographies
PS = American Revolution: Primary Sources

A

Abolitionism
  B *1:* 47–48, 50–51, 134; *2:* 382
Acadians
  B *1:* 152
Account of European Settlement in America, An
  B *1:* 82
Account of the Bilious Remitting Yellow Fever, An
  B *2:* 431
Acrostic
  PS 205, 207
Adams, Abigail
  A 75, 88, 134–35, 135 (ill.)
  B *1:* **1–8,** 1 (ill.), 18; *2:* 343
  PS 48, 125, 145, 145 (ill.), 146
Adams, Charles Francis
  PS 132
Adams, Elizabeth "Betsy" Wells
  B *1:* 22
Adams, Elizabeth Checkley
  B *1:* 21, 22
Adams, Hannah
  B *2:* 340, 341

Adams, Henry
  B *2:* 307
Adams, John
  A 34, 39, 39 (ill.), 65, 75–76, 87–89, 94, 118, 131–35, 185
  B *1:* **9–19,** 9 (ill.), 11 (ill.), 29, 49, 109, 124, 188, 194, 201, 251–52, 255; *2:* 343, 428, 431–32, 471
  PS 2, 17, 22, 36, 43, 47 (ill.), 48, 87, 104–6, 108, 123, 124 (ill.), 124, 125, 126, 131, 132, 135–38, 145, 146, 148, 152, 166–67, 179, 186
Adams, John (father of President John Adams)
  B *1:* 9
Adams, John Quincy
  B *1:* 18; *2:* 273
  PS 123
Adams, Mary Fifield
  B *1:* 20
Adams, Peter
  B *1:* 9
Adams, Samuel
  A 49 (ill.), 50, 53, 57, 59, 65, 70, 74–75

B *1:* **20–30**, 20 (ill.), 27 (ill.), 108, 144, 201, 204; *2:* 359, 429, 444

PS 4, 17, 29, 32–33, 33 (ill.), 34, 35, 41, 42, 43, 87–88, 148, 172, 174, 178, 179, 186, 188 (ill.), 213

Adams, Susanna Boylston
  B *1:* 9

Administration of Justice Act
  PS 39, 212

Admiralty courts
  PS 8, 27

Adulateur, The
  B *2:* 473

"African Slavery in America"
  PS 100

Age of Enlightenment
  B *2:* 354

Age of Reason
  B *2:* 358

Agricola
  B *1:* 102

Albany, New York
  B *2:* 329

Albany Plan of Union
  B *1:* 118

Aldridge, A. Owen
  B *2:* 357

Alexander Hamilton, American
  B *1:* 189

Alexandria, Virginia
  B *2:* 313

Alien and Sedition Acts
  B *1:* 17, 252, 253

Allen, Ethan
  A 83–84, 103
  B *1:* **31–37**, 31 (ill.), 33 (ill.)

Allen, Gay Wilson
  B *1:* 98

Allen, Ira
  B *1:* 35, 36

Allen, Joseph
  B *1:* 31

Allen, Mary Baker
  B *1:* 31

Allen, Mary Bronson
  B *1:* 32, 36

Allison, Robert J.
  B *1:* 102

Amelia (princess)
  PS 59

American Civil War
  B *1:* 214
  PS 116, 147

American Department
  PS 30

American Eras: The Revolutionary Era, 1754–1783
  B *1:* 102

"American Independence, an Everlasting Deliverance from British Tyranny"
  B *2:* 333

American Moral Reform Society
  B *1:* 51

American Philosophical Society
  B *1:* 117; *2:* 346

American Prohibition Act
  PS 60–61

American Psychiatric Association
  B *2:* 432

American soldiers
  A 173 (ill.)
  B *2:* 374, 445, 483

American Times, The
  B *2:* 351

André, John
  A 141
  B *1:* 41 (ill.), 43 (ill.), 235; *2:* 349
  PS 204, 204 (ill.), 205, 205 (ill.), 209

Anne (queen)
  B *1:* 156

Annual Register
  B *1:* 82; *2:* 331
  PS 51

Anti–tax movements
  B *2:* 443, 446–449

Arcadians
  B *1:* 150

Arlington, Massachusetts
  B *1:* 93

Arlington National Cemetery
  B *2:* 280

Armistead, James
  A 123

Arnold, Benedict
  A 106, 141, 161, 179, 181
  B *1:* **38–45**, 41 (ill.); *2:* 349
  PS 170, **203–10**, 204 (ill.), 208

Arnold, Benjamin
  B *1:* 33

Arnold, Margaret Mansfield
  B *1:* 39
Arnold, Margaret Shippen
  B *1:* 41, 44
Articles of Confederation
  A 118
  B *1:* 28, 190, 225, 242;
    2: 317, 485
  PS **151–68**, 251
Ashburn, Joseph
  B *2:* 419
Ashburn, Lucilla
  B *2:* 423
Asselinau, Roger
  B *1:* 98
Assembly of New York
  PS 65
Associated Loyalists
  B *2:* 349
Association of Philadelphia
  B *2:* 387, 388
Astor, John Jacob
  B *2:* 277
Atlanta Constitution
  B *1:* 216
Attucks, Crispus
  A 121, 122 (ill.)
  B *1:* 46 (ill.), **48–49**, 49 (ill.)
Augusta, Georgia
  B *1:* 213
Augusta (princess)
  B *1:* 155

B

Bache, Sarah Franklin
  B *1:* 117; *2:* 388
Bacon, Delia
  B *2:* 333
Bahamas
  B *1:* 153
Ballyduff, Ireland
  B *1:* 81
Baltimore, Lord
  PS 84
Baltimore, Maryland
  A 148
Bank of the United States
  B *1:* 193
Barlow, Joel
  A 34
  B *2:* 333

Barnard, John
  B *1:* 200
Barré, Isaac
  B *2:* 504
  PS 17
Bastille, The
  B *2:* 269, 287, 289
Batherick, "Mother"
  B *1:* 93
Battle of Bunker Hill
  A 32, 85–88, 85 (ill.), 97 (ill.),
    100
  B *1:* 48, 52
  PS 127
Battle of Long Island
  A 140
Battles of Lexington and Concord
  A 78 (ill.), 79–84, 79 (ill.),
    82 (ill.)
  B *1:* 108, 144, 145
  PS 127, 128 (ill.), 213 (ill.)
Belcher, Jonathan
  PS 35
Bemis Heights, New York
  B *2:* 259
Bennington, Vermont
  A 160
  B *1:* 37
Benton, Thomas Hart
  B *1:* 210
Berlin, Germany
  B *2:* 400, 407
Bernard, Francis
  PS 15, 30, 31, 41, 44, 174, 178
Bible
  B *1:* 61; *2:* 341
Bill for the More General
    Diffusion of Knowledge
  B *1:* 249
Bill of Rights
  B *1:* 226; *2:* 302, 306, 318,
    319, 474
Billings, William
  A 34
Binger, Carl
  B *2:* 427, 431
Binney, Barnabas
  B *2:* 438, 439
Black Freedom Fighters
  B *1:* **46–53**
Blacks in the American
    Revolution
  A 100–101, 107, 115–26,
    120 (ill.), 134, 137, 161, 177

B *1:* 93, **46–53**, 151, 152;
  2: 381
Blackstone, William
  A 13, 13 (ill.)
Bladensburg, Maryland
  B *2:* 275, 281
Bloodletting
  B *2:* 430
Bonaparte, Napoleon
  B *2:* 261, 271, 272
"Bonnie Prince Charlie."
  See Stuart, Charles Edward
Book publishing in
    Colonial America
  B *2:* 409, 416
Booth, Sallie Smith
  B *1:* 214
Boston Athenaeum
  B *2:* 341
Boston Committee
    of Correspondence
  B *2:* 393
Boston Federal Street Theatre
  B *2:* 343
Boston Intelligence
  B *2:* 398
Boston Latin School
  B *1:* 198
Boston Library Society
  B *2:* 398
Boston, Massachusetts
  A 141
  B *1:* 10, 12, 28–29, 33, 101,
    143–44, 159, 180, 199–200,
    203, 205, 208, 231; *2:* 340,
    391–92, 395, 404, 483, 504
  PS 40–41, 171–82, 183–89
Boston Massacre
  A 58–60, 58 (ill.), 121
  B *1:* 12, 24, 48, 49, 202; *2:* 393
  PS 31 (ill.), 34, 35, 179
Boston Port Act
  PS 39, 40, 41, 44–45, 212
Boston, Seige of
  A 103, 141
Boston Tea Party
  A 65–67, 65 (ill.)
  B *1:* 12, 25, 142, 159, 188;
    2: 368, 394, 452, 470–71, 504
  PS 33, 38 (ill.), 39, 179, 201
Boston Town Committee
  B *1:* 202
Bowdoin, James
  B *1:* 207

Boycotts
  A 48, 51, 54
  B *1:* 203
Boynton, Percy H.
  B *2:* 351
Braddock, Edward
  B *1:* 166
Braintree, Massachusetts
  B *1:* 9
Brandywine Creek, Pennsylvania
  B *1:* 233; *2:* 485
Brant, Isaac
  B *1:* 56
Brant, Joseph
  A 118–19, 119 (ill.)
  B *1:* **54–62**, 54 (ill.), 60 (ill.),
    65, 68, 69, 170
Brant, Mary "Molly"
  B *1:* 55, 57, **63–70**, 64 (ill.)
Brant, Nicklaus
  B *1:* 64
Breed's Hill, Massachusetts
  A 85–86
  B *1:* 145; *2:* 444
Bride of Fort Edward, The
  B *2:* 333
"Britannicus"
  B *2:* 348
British Army
  PS 31
British Royal Navy
  A 111–12
  PS 30
British taxation of American
    colonies
  B *1:* 11, 22–24, 84, 86, 105–7,
    157, 159, 160, 188, 199,
    219; *2:* 302, 314, 356, 361,
    364, 366, 368, 394, 411,
    428, 465, 482
Brom and Bett v. J. Ashley Esq.
  B *1:* 132
Brook, John
  B *1:* 160
Brookhiser, Richard
  B *1:* 189–91
Brooklyn, New York
  B *2:* 277
Brookneal, Virginia
  B *1:* 226
Brown, Caesar
  A 100
Brunswick, Georgia
  B *1:* 216

Buchanan, Frances
  B *1:* 36
Bunker Hill, Massachusetts
  B *1:* 145, 231; *2:* 444
Burgoyne, John
  A 96, 96 (ill.), 116, 118, 157,
    159–64, 167
  B *1:* 40, **71–80,** 71 (ill.), 77
    (ill.), 231, 233; *2:* 260, 329,
    331, 333, 400, 402, 444
"Burgoyne's Offensive"
  A 159–60
  B *1:* 78; *2:* 401
Burke, Edmund
  A 73
  B *1:* **81–89,** 81 (ill.);
    2: 332, 382
  PS **49–54,** 50 (ill.), 86–87,
    104, 124
Burke, Jane Nugent
  B *1:* 83
Burke, Richard
  B *1:* 88
Burke, William
  B *1:* 82
Burlington Committee of Safety
  B *2:* 347
Burlington, New Jersey
  B *2:* 346, 347
Burlington, Vermont
  B *1:* 31, 37
Burr, Aaron
  B *1:* 194, 195
Bushnell, David
  A 141

C

"Call to Arms, The"
  A 81 (ill.)
Calvert, George
  PS 84
Cambridge flag
  B *2:* 419
Cambridge, Massachusetts
  B *1:* 10, 13, 21, 198
Camp followers
  A 110
  B *1:* 91; *2:* 401
Campbell, Archibald
  B *1:* 34
Canada
  A 159
  B *1:* 239

Canadian Campaign
  A 159
Canby, William
  B *2:* 418
Capitol Rotunda
  B *2:* 280
Carleton, Guy
  A 157, 159
  B *1:* 78; *2:* 349
  PS 248
Carlos III (king)
  B *1:* 148
Caroll, Philip Henry
  B *2:* 335
Castle Island
  B *2:* 396
Castle of Otranto
  B *2:* 464
  PS 245
Cavalry
  B *2:* 374, 375
Chairman of the Board of War
  B *1:* 15
Chamber pot
  A 62 (ill.)
Charles II (king)
  PS 58
Charles III (king)
  B *1:* 149
Charles X (king)
  B *2:* 272
Charles River
  A 86
Charleston, South Carolina
  A 105, 174, 177
  B *2:* 260, 377, 380
  PS 236, 236 (ill.)
Charlestown, Massachusetts
  A 85
Charlotte Sophia (queen)
  B *1:* 157
  PS 58
Charlottesville, Virginia
  B *1:* 246, 250; *2:* 405
Cherokee
  A 116
Cherry Valley (New York)
    Massacre
  A 117–19, 117 (ill.)
  B *1:* 58, 59
Chicago, Illinois
  B *2:* 432
Children's literature
  A 30

Choctaw
  B *1:* 151, 152
Christ Church Burial Ground
  B *2:* 432
Christianity
  A 2
  B *1:* 63; *2:* 354
Church of England
  A 2
Cincinnatus
  B *2:* 277
Civil War. *See* American Civil War
Clanranald, Lady
  B *2:* 294
Clark, George Rogers
  B *2:* 313
Clark, William
  B *2:* 431
Clay, Henry
  B *1:* 210
Claypoole, Clarissa Sidney
  B *2:* 423
Claypoole, Harriet
  B *2:* 423
Claypoole, Jane
  B *2:* 423
Claypoole, John
  B *2:* 422, 423
Claypoole, Rachel
  B *2:* 423
Claypoole, Susan
  B *2:* 423
Clinton, Henry
  A 96, 171, 172 (ill.), 173–74,
    177, 179, 181, 183
  B *1:* 43, 231, 233, 235;
    2: 348, 349
  PS 235, 236, 238
"The Club"
  B *1:* 83
Clyne, Patricia Edwards
  B *1:* 93
Cobbitt, William
  B *2:* 359
Coercive Acts
  A 67
Cohn, Art
  PS 209
College du Plessis
  B *2:* 265
College of New Jersey
  B *2:* 426
College of William and Mary
  B *1:* 246

"Colonial Gazette, The"
  A 185 (ill.)
Colonialism
  A 1
Colonies, thirteen
  A 128 (ill.)
  PS 2
"Columbiad, The"
  B *2:* 333
Committee of Five
  A 132
  PS 136, 146
Committee on the State of the
    Northern Army
  B *1:* 28
Committees of correspondence
  A 70
  B *2:* 314
  PS 32, 33, 113
Common Sense
  A 35, 101 (ill.), 102–3
  B *2:* 355, 428
  PS 61, **97–106**, 99 (ill.), 229
Commonwealth of Virginia
  B *2:* 316
Concord, Massachusetts
  A 79–81, 83, 86
  B *1:* 28, 144, 223, 231;
    2: 394, 395, 444, 482
Congratulation, The
  B *2:* 350
"Constantia"
  B *2:* 339
Constitution of the United States.
    See U.S. Constitution
Constitutional Convention
  B *2:* 305, 485, 486
Continental Army
  A 83, 89, 93–94, 96, 99–101,
    107, 115, 119–20, 130–31,
    140, 145–46, 149, 153, 169,
    182–83, 185–86
  B *1:* 13, 14, 17, 28, 34, 111,
    189, 206, 212, 223; *2:* 259,
    265, 276, 315, 328, 332, 356,
    403, 418, 420, 422, 428, 483
  PS 101, 214, 221, 222, 224
Continental Association
  A 77
  PS **111–26**
Continental colors
  B *2:* 419

Continental Congress. *See also*
  First Contintental Congress;
  Second Continental
  Congress
  A 148–49, 158, 178
  B *1:* 35, 47, 190, 191, 224;
  2: 265, 303, 315, 348, 350,
  381, 412, 428, 482
Continental navy
  A 111
Convention of Virginia
  B *1:* 221
Conway, Thomas
  B *2:* 429
Conway's Cabal
  A 164
  B *2:* 428
Copley, John Singleton
  A 38
  B *1:* 205
Corbin, John
  B *1:* 90, 91
Corbin, Margaret Cochran
  A 110
  B *1:* **90–96**; *2:* 323
Cornwallis, Charles
  A 145, 176, 176 (ill.), 179,
  181–83
  B *2:* 267, 485
  PS 237 (ill.), 238
Cou, Anne de
  B *2:* 347
Creoles
  B *1:* 149, 152
Cresswell, Nicholas
  A 104, 151
Crèvecoeur, Hector St. Jean de
  B *1:* 97 (ill.), **97–104**
Crisis, The
  B *2:* 356
  PS 98–99, **229–34**
Cross Creek, North Carolina
  B *2:* 300
Crown Point, New York
  B *1:* 33
Cuba
  B *1:* 153
Cumberland, Duke of
  B *2:* 296
Currency Act
  A 46
Cushing, Thomas
  PS 184, 185

Custis, George Washington Parke
  B *2:* 280
Custis–Lee Mansion
  B *2:* 280
Customs officials
  PS 30 (ill.), 30

D

Dabney, Austin
  A 125
Danbury, Connecticut
  B *1:* 40
Dandridge, Dorothea
  B *1:* 225
Dandridge, Francis
  PS 12
Darragh, Lydia
  B *1:* 66, 67
Dartmouth, Lord
  PS 196
Daughters of the American
  Revolution
  B *1:* 177, 216
Dawes, William
  A 80
  B *1:* 144; *2:* 395
  PS 213
Day, Luke
  B *2:* 448
Deane, Silas
  B *2:* 258, 373
  PS 43, 139
Declaration and Resolves
  A 77
Declaration of Independence
  A 77, 134
  B *1:* 14, 18, 28, 110, 120, 174,
  176, 198, 205, 224, 232, 239,
  248, 255; *2:* 269, 303, 314,
  426, 428
  PS 59, **135–49**, 141 (ill.),
  144 (ill.)
Declaration of Martial Law
  PS 214, **217–20**
Declaration of Rights and
  Grievances
  PS 15
Declaration of the Causes and
  Necessity of Taking Up Arms
  A 89
  PS **127–33**

Declaration of the Rights of Man
and the Citizen
B *2:* 290
Declarations of Rights and Privileges
B *1:* 107
Declaratory Act
A 50
B *1:* 158
PS **19–23**
Defeat, The
B *2:* 473
Deism
B *2:* 354, 359
Delaware River (crossing)
A 146–47, 150
B *2:* 279
PS 230 (ill.)
Democratic Party
B *1:* 17
Democratic-Republicans
B *2:* 487
Department of the Treasury.
See U.S. Department of
the Treasury
Dick, William
B *2:* 298
Dickinson College
B *1:* 112; *2:* 431
PS 70
Dickinson, John
A 35, 36 (ill.), 52, 54, 75, 87
B *1:* 105 (ill.), **105–13,**
188, 205
PS 42, **63–70,** 64 (ill.), 128,
131, 132, 146, 151, 166, 167
Dickinson, Mary Cadwalader
B *1:* 105
Dickinson, Mary Norris
B *1:* 108
Dickinson, Philomen
B *1:* 110
Dickinson, Samuel
B *1:* 105
Dickinson, Temperance
B *2:* 345
Digges, William Dudley
B *2:* 281, 282
"Direct" tax
A 47
District of Columbia
B *2:* 278
Donaldson, Sarah Ross
B *2:* 423

Dorchester Heights,
Massachusetts
A 85
Dover, Delaware
B *1:* 106
Duane, John
B *1:* 108
Dublin, Ireland
B *1:* 81
Dunmore, Lord
A 123
B *1:* 167, 220–23
PS 87, 89, 95, 214,
217–20, 235
Dunmore's War
B *1:* 167–68

E

Earl of Strafford
PS 243–44
*Early Abridgement of the History of
England, The*
B *1:* 82
East India Company
A 64
PS 37, 39, 179, 201
"Edict by the King of Prussia, An"
PS **71–80**
Edinburgh, Scotland
B *2:* 295, 426
Education
A 21, 21 (ill.)
*Eighteenth-Century Travels in
Pennsylvania and New York*
B *1:* 103
Electricity
PS 74
Elizabeth II (queen)
PS 61
*Encyclopedia of the American
Revolution*
B *1:* 159
Erasmus Academy
B *2:* 277
Ethopian Regiment
PS 219
"Extracts from Virginia Charters,
with Some Remarks upon
Them"
B *2:* 314

F

Fairfax County Court
  B *2:* 313, 319
Fairfax County, Virginia
  B *2:* 312
"Fairfax Resolves"
  B *2:* 314
Fairfield, Connecticut
  B *1:* 205
Fallen Timbers
  B *2:* 487
Families, colonial
  A 20 (ill.)
Faneuil Hall
  B *1:* 27 (ill.)
Farewell Address to the Armies of
    the United States
  PS 247–53
Farming
  A 2, 2 (ill.), 17
Fashion, colonial
  A 8 (ill.), 9 (ill.)
"Father of American Psychiatry"
  B *2:* 432
Faubius
  B *1:* 112
Federal Constitutional
    Convention
  B *2:* 312, 317, 319
Federalist, The
  B *1:* 243; *2:* 305
Federalist Papers
  B *1:* 187, 191
Federalist Party
  B *1:* 16–18, 194, 226; *2:* 306,
    310–11, 487
Finley, Samuel
  B *2:* 426
First Continental Congress. *See
    also* Continental Congress;
    Second Continental
    Congress
  A 74–75, 75 (ill.), 77
  B *1:* 26, 108, 161, 188, 203,
    220, 239; *2:* 386, 394, 482
  PS 51, 57, 89, 97, 108–10,
    111–26, 122 (ill.), 124, 126
First Philadelphia Battalion
  B *1:* 110
Fletcher, Rachel Ross
  B *2:* 417
Florida
  B *1:* 153

Flower, Milton E.
  B *1:* 106
Food, colonial
  A 18 (ill.)
Foreign soldiers in the
    American Revolution
  B *2:* 258, 404
Fort Ann, New York
  B *2:* 330
Fort Edward, New York
  A 160
  B *2:* 329–30, 333, 335
Fort George, New York
  B *2:* 401
Fort Henry, Virginia
  B *1:* 215
Fort Lee, New Jersey
  A 145
Fort Mifflin
  B *2:* 279
Fort Ticonderoga, New York
  A 83–84, 103, 160
  B *1:* 31, 33, 141
Fort Washington, New York
  A 145
  B *2:* 281, 323
Forten, James
  B *1:* 46, 50 (ill.), **50–51**
Fowler, William M., Jr.
  B *1:* 199
Fradin, Dennis
  B *1:* 206
France in the American
    Revolution
  A 153, 158, 165–66, 168, 173,
    177, 182–83
  B *1:* 150; *2:* 288, 377, 415, 444,
    465, 485
Franklin and Marshall College
  B *2:* 431
Franklin, Benjamin
  A 29, 30, 33, 33 (ill.), 52, 62,
    78, 89, 99, 118, 132–34,
    165–66, 165 (ill.), 185
  B *1:* 14–15, 101, 114 (ill.),
    114–24, 121 (ill.), 125–26,
    128 (ill.), 248, 251; *2:* 288,
    346, 350, 355, 359, 373, 427
  PS 9–10, 19–20, 21, 27, 35, 43,
    69, **71–80**, 73 (ill.), 78 (ill.),
    135–36, 123, 152, 170,
    183–89, 196, **197–201**,
    198 (ill.)

Franklin, Deborah Read
  B *1:* 116–17, 120, 125 (ill.),
    125–30, 128 (ill.)
Franklin, Francis Folger
  · **B** *1:* 117
Franklin, James
  B *1:* 116
Franklin stove
  PS 74
Franklin, William
  B *1:* 126, 127; *2:* 346, 349
  PS 77
Fraser, Simon
  B *2:* 329
Frederick II (king)
  B *2:* 404
  PS 71, 72 (ill.)
Frederick Louis (prince of Wales)
  B *1:* 155
Frederick the Great (king)
  A 153–54
  PS 71, 72 (ill.)
Frederick William II (king)
  B *2:* 399
Fredericton, New Brunswick,
    Canada
  B *2:* 345, 352
Freedom of the press
  B *2:* 499
Freeman, Elizabeth
  B *1:* 131 (ill.), **131–37**
Freeman's Farm
  A 161
French and Indian War
  A 45, 87, 95, 106
  B *1:* 22, 31, 39, 55, 72, 98, 139,
    166–67, 229; *2:* 313, 361,
    364, 392, 456, 480, 482
  PS 2–3, 82
French Declaration of the Rights
    of Man and the Citizen
  B *2:* 269
French Legion of Honor
  B *2:* 271
French Revolution
  B *1:* 85, 87, 88, 97, 103; *2:* 269,
    272, 281, 286, 353
  PS 99
Freneau, Philip
  A 153
  B *2:* 333
Fritz, Jean
  B *1:* 199

Fugitive Slave Law
  B *1:* 134
Fulton, Robert
  B *2:* 397

G

Gage, Thomas
  A 67, 74, 80, 84–86, 96, 109
  B *1:* 75–76, **138–46,** 138 (ill.),
    202, 231
  PS 26, 31, 35, 39–40, 44,
    46–47, 65, 173, 200, 212, 213
Galloway, Joseph
  A 75
Gálvez, Bernardo de
  B *1:* **147–54,** 147 (ill.)
Gates, Horatio
  A 161, 163
  B *2:* 259, 332, 402, 429
Gault, Charlayne Hunter
  PS 105
*Gentleman's and Lady's Town and
    Country Magazine*
  B *2:* 339
George I (king)
  B *1:* 156; *2:* 295
George II (king)
  B *1:* 155, 156; *2:* 295, 362
  PS 7, 58
George III (king)
  A 44, 47, 53, 61–62, 68, 73, 77,
    84, 90, 93, 99, 101–2, 123,
    127, 133, 184, 187
  B *1:* 15, 27, 43, 75, 84, 93,
    108–9, 120, **155–63,** 155
    (ill.), 158 (ill.), 199, 202, 205,
    221, 229, 239, 247; *2:* 299,
    314, 347, 355, 365, 400, 404,
    412, 457, 501, 502, 505
  PS 3, 7, 16–17, 20, 22, 44, 47,
    51, **55–62,** 56 (ill.), 82, 84,
    85–86, 92, 108, 109, 112 (ill.),
    113, 122, 127, 128, 130, 138,
    147, 173, 192, 200, 212, 241,
    245, 247–48
George IV (king)
  B *1:* 162
  PS 59
Georgia
  PS 16, 108, 122, 138
Germain, Lord
  B *2:* 403

German soldiers
  B *2:* 363, 483
Germantown, Pennsylvania
  B *1:* 93, 233
Gerry, Elbridge
  B *1:* 208
Girty, Simon
  B *1:* 164 (ill.), **164–72**
"Give me liberty, or give me
    death" speech
  PS 89–96, 217
Gleaner, The
  B *2:* 339, 343
Gloucester, Massachusetts
  B *2:* 338, 339, 344
"God Save the King"
  B *1:* 157
Goddard, Mary Katherine
  B *1:* **173–77**
  PS 147
Goddard, Sarah Updike
  B *1:* 173, 175
Gordon riots
  B *2:* 505
Gottschalk, Louis R.
  B *2:* 268
Gracie Mansion
  B *2:* 277
Granary Burying Ground
  B *2:* 398
Grand River, Ontario
  B *1:* 54
Grant, Jehu
  B *1:* 46, **51**
Grant, Ulysses S.
  PS 42
Graydon, Alexander
  A 140
  B *1:* 34
Great Lakes
  A 41
Green Mountain Boys
  A 83–84
  B *1:* 32, 34, 37
Greene, Nathanael
  A 145, 179
  B *2:* 260
  PS 204
Grenville, George
  B *1:* 157; *2:* 363–64, 457
  PS 7–8, 16, 17, 42
Grenville, Richard
  B *2:* 363, 364

Grimm, Friedrick-Melchior von
  B *1:* 103
Griscom, Deborah
  B *2:* 423
Griscom, Samuel
  B *2:* 417
Group, The
  B *2:* 473
Gunston Hall
  B *2:* 313, 317, 319

H

Hale, Nathan
  A 141
  B *1:* 178 (ill.), **178–86**, 182 (ill.)
Halifax, Nova Scotia, Canada
  A 136
Halifax, Virginia
  B *2:* 300
Hallowell, Mr.
  PS 172
Hamilton, Alexander
  B *1:* 17, 18, 187 (ill.), 188 (ill.),
    187–97, 242, 251; *2:* 277,
    307, 487
Hamilton, Angelica
  B *1:* 196
Hamilton, Eliza
  B *1:* 196
Hamilton, Elizabeth Schuyler
  B *1:* 189
Hamilton, James
  B *1:* 187
Hamilton, Philip
  B *1:* 196
"Hamiltonian System"
  B *1:* 192
Hancock, Dorothy Quincy
  B *1:* 205
Hancock, John
  A 46, 84
  B *1:* 27, 29, 144, 160, 198 (ill.),
    198–209, 203 (ill.); *2:* 343,
    440, 444
  PS 22, 30, 87–88, 126, 146,
    147 (ill.), 148, 172, 174, 175,
    178, 213
Hanoverians
  B *2:* 295
Harper's Monthly
  B *2:* 419

Harrison, Benjamin
  B *1:* 205
Hart, Benjamin
  B *1:* 210
Hart, John
  B *1:* 216
Hart, Nancy Morgan
  B *1:* **210–17**, 213 (ill.)
Hart, Sukey
  B *1:* 213
Hartford, Connecticut
  B *2:* 311
Harvard College
  A 22 (ill.)
Harvard University
  B *1:* 10, 21, 198
Havana, Cuba
  B *1:* 151
Hawke, David Freeman
  B *2:* 429
Hawthorne, Nigel
  PS 61
Hayes, Cuff
  A 100
Hays, William
  B *2:* 322–24
Hendrickson, Robert
  B *1:* 189, 192
Henry, John
  B *1:* 218
Henry, Patrick
  A 47, 75
  B *1:* 107, 218 (ill.), **218–27**,
     222 (ill.), 249; *2:* 303, 314,
     319, 428–29
  PS 13–14, **89–96**, 114, 214,
     217
Henry, Sarah Shelton
  B *1:* 218
Henry, Sarah Winston Syme
  B *1:* 218, 221
Hessians
  A 102, 136, 138, 140, 142–43,
     147, 151 (ill.), 159–60, 162,
     174, 183–84, 187
Highlanders
  B *2:* 296, 299
Hill, Wills
  PS 30
History of the American Revolution
  B *2:* 333, 382
History of the Jews, A
  B *2:* 340

*History of the Revolution of South
  Carolina*
  B *2:* 382
*History of the Rise, Progress and
  Termination of the American
  Revolution, The*
  B *2:* 475
History of the United States
  B *2:* 384
Hitchcock, Enos
  B *2:* 342
House of Burgesses. *See* Virginia
  House of Burgesses
House of Delegates
  B *1:* 225
Howe, Richard
  A 136, 138
  B *1:* 232, 235
Howe, William
  A 86, 96, 104, 123, 129–30,
     136, 136 (ill.), 138, 141, 144,
     145 (ill.), 146, 151, 157–58,
     160, 167–68
  B *1:* 76, 145, 183, **228–36**,
     228 (ill.); *2:* 402, 403, 412
  PS 152, 153 (ill.)
Hoyt, Edwin P.
  B *1:* 34
Hudson Falls, New York
  B *2:* 335
Hughes, John
  PS 10
Hutchinson, Anne
  PS 173
Hutchinson letters affair
  PS 44, 170, **171–82**, **183–89**,
     191–96, **197–201**
Hutchinson, Thomas
  A 52, 65
  PS 32, 44, 169–70, **171–82**,
     183–89, **191–96**, 192 (ill.),
     197–201

I

Independence Day
  B *1:* 14
Indian uprisings
  A 42
Indian warfare
  A 117–18
Indians. *See also* Native
  Americans
  PS 3, 164, 165 (ill.)

Influenza
    B *1:* 159
Ingersoll, Jared
    PS 10
*Inscription for a Curious Chamber
        Stove*
    B *2:* 350
Inspector General of the U.S.
        Army
    B *1:* 194
Intolerable Acts
    A 67, 69–70, 73, 79
    B *1:* 12, 75, 202, 203, 221, 239;
        2: 368, 504
    PS **37–48**, 200, 212

J

J. C. B.
    B *2:* 334
Jacobins
    B *2:* 270
Jacobites
    B *2:* 295, 298
Jamaica
    B *1:* 153
Jamaica Plains, Massachusetts
    B *2:* 395
James I (king)
    A 1
James II (king)
    B *1:* 142 (ill.); *2:* 295
Jamestown, Virginia
    A 2
    PS 1
Jay, John
    A 76, 185
    B *1:* 15, 191, 237 (ill.), **237–45**,
        243 (ill.); *2:* 304, 351
    PS 123
Jay, Sally
    B *1:* 240
Jay, Sarah
    B *1:* 238
Jay's Treaty
    B *1:* 244
Jefferson, Jane Randolph
    B *1:* 246
Jefferson, Martha Wales Skelton
    B *1:* 250
Jefferson, Peter
    B *1:* 246

Jefferson, Thomas
    A 7, 61, 70 (ill.), 84, 132–34,
        132 (ill.)
    B *1:* 14, 16, 18, 29, 101, 112,
        121, 160, 192, 194, 220,
        224–26, 246 (ill.), 248 (ill.),
        246–55; *2:* 262, 268, 271,
        278, 306, 307, 316, 319, 358,
        405, 428, 431, 432
    PS 17, 33, 42, **81–88**, 114–15,
        128, 137 (ill.), 137, 138,
        146, 154
Johnson, Chrisfield
    B *2:* 334
Johnson, Samuel
    B *1:* 83
Johnson, William
    B *1:* 64, 65, 68
Jones, David
    B *2:* 329
Jones, John Paul
    A 111 (ill.), 112
Jones, Thomas
    A 146
Journal of Events
    B *1:* 24
*Journal of Nicholas Cresswell, The:
        1774–1777*
    A 104
*Journal of the Reign of George III
        from 1771 to 1783*
    B *2:* 465
Jusserand, J. J.
    B *2:* 280

K

Kemble, Margaret
    B *1:* 140
Kentucky Resolutions
    B *1:* 253
Kettle Creek, Georgia
    B *1:* 211
Kilbride, Scotland
    B *2:* 297
Kilmuir, Scotland
    B *2:* 301
King Carlos III. *See* Carlos III
        (king)
King Charles II. *See* Charles II
        (king)
King Charles III. *See* Charles III
        (king)

King Charles X. *See* Charles X
  (king)
King Frederick II. *See* Frederick II
  (king)
King George II. *See* George II (king)
King George III. *See* George III
  (king)
King George IV. *See* George IV
  (king)
King, Hannah Waterman
  B *1:* 38
King James I. *See* James I (king)
King James II. *See* James II (king)
King Louis XVI. *See* Louis XVI
  (king)
King Louis XVII. *See* Louis XVII
  (king)
King Louis XVIII. *See* Louis XVIII
  (king)
King Philip's War
  A 3
King's Chapel
  B *2:* 397
Kingsburgh, Scotland
  B *2:* 301
Kite, Elizabeth S.
  B *2:* 281
Knowlton, Thomas
  B *1:* 181
Knowlton's Rangers
  B *1:* 181
Knox, Henry
  A 103, 137, 150
  B *2:* 487
Kosciuszko, Thaddeus
  B *2:* 257 (ill.), **257–63**

L

Lafayette, Adrienne de
  B *2:* 271
Lafayette, Anastasie de
  B *2:* 271
Lafayette, George Washington de
  B *2:* 271
Lafayette, Henriette de
  B *2:* 271
Lafayette, James
  A 123
Lafayette, Marquis de
  A 123, 158, 177, 181
  B *2:* 264 (ill.), **264–74**,
    267 (ill.), 374, 445

Lafayette, Virginie de
  B *2:* 271
Lagrange, France
  B *2:* 271
Lake Champlain Maritime
  Museum
  PS 209
Lambert, Mary
  B *2:* 354
Lamington, New Jersey
  B *2:* 328
Land Bank
  PS 35
Lane, Anna Maria
  B *1:* 93
Lane, John
  B *1:* 93
LaNotre, André
  B *2:* 275
Laurens, Henry
  B *2:* 381
Lauterbach Castle
  B *2:* 406, 407
Lavien, John
  B *1:* 187
Lavien, Rachel Fawcitt
  B *1:* 187
Lee, Arthur
  PS 41, 42–43
Lee, Charles
  A 94, 100, 148–49
  PS 124, 224
Lee, Charles Henry
  B *2:* 259
Lee, Francis Lightfoot
  PS 42
Lee, Henry "Light-Horse Harry"
  B *1:* 193; *2:* 259
  PS 42
Lee, Richard Bland
  PS 43
Lee, Richard Henry
  A 75, 131
  B *1:* 220, 223, 224, 226; *2:* 429
  PS 42, 113, 114, 115 (ill.),
    135, 151
Lee, Robert E.
  PS 42
Lee's resolution
  A 131, 134
L'Enfant, Pierre Charles
  B *2:* 275 (ill.), **275–83**,
    278 (ill.)

Lennon, Sarah
  PS 58
Letter to George Washington
  B *2:* 358
Letter to the Earl of Strafford
    about the Surrender of
    Cornwallis at Yorktown
  PS **241–45**
*Letters and Memoirs Relating to the
    War of American Independence*
  B *2:* 407
Letters, and Sketches of Sermons
  B *2:* 343
*Letters from a Farmer in
    Pennsylvania to the
    Inhabitants of the British
    Colonies*
  B *1:* 107
  PS 42, **63–70**, 131, 132
Letters from an American Farmer
  B *1:* 99
Lewis and Clark expedition
  B *1:* 254; *2:* 431
Lewis, Anthony
  PS 105
Lewis, Meriwether
  B *2:* 431
Lexington, Massachusetts
  A 79–81, 83, 86
  B *1:* 28, 204; *2:* 394, 395, 444
Liberia
  A 125
Liberty Bowl
  B *2:* 393
Liberty (ship)
  B *1:* 3, 5–8, 200
  PS 30, 126, 172, 178
Liberty Tree
  B *1:* 200
Library of Congress
  B *1:* 254
  PS 154, 155
Lightning rod
  PS 74
Lincoln, Benjamin
  A 174
  B *2:* 405, 449
Litchfield, Connecticut
  B *1:* 31
Literacy
  A 30, 37
Little Egg Harbor, New Jersey
  B *2:* 375

Livingston, Robert
  A 132
  B *1:* 14
  PS 135–36, 136 (ill.), 146
Livingston, William
  B *1:* 110
Logan, James
  B *1:* 169
London, England
  B *1:* 38, 43, 99, 106, 199;
    2: 340, 358, 394, 427
London Magazine
  PS 70
Long Island, New York
  A 138, 141
  B *1:* 189, 232
Longfellow, Henry Wadsworth
  B *2:* 391, 395
Loring, Elizabeth
  B *1:* 232
Louis XVI (king)
  A 166–67
  B *1:* 87; *2:* 265, 270, 272,
    276, 284 (ill.), **284–93**,
    292 (ill.), 373
  PS 99
Louis XVII (king)
  B *2:* 272
Louis XVIII (king)
  B *2:* 272
Louisiana
  B *1:* 149, 150, 153
Louisiana Purchase
  B *1:* 253; *2:* 307
  PS 137
*Loyal Verses of Joseph Stansbury and
    Doctor Jonathan Odell, The*
  B *2:* 348
Loyalists
  A 37, 98, 104–5, 107, 118, 127,
    130, 138, 146, 172, 177
  B *1:* 13, 211, 233, 239, 244
Lyman, Simeon
  A 100

M

Macdonald, Alexander
  B *2:* 300
Macdonald, Alexander of Sleat
  B *2:* 297
Macdonald, Allan
  B *2:* 298, 300

Macdonald, Angus
   B *2:* 294
Macdonald, Flora
   B *2:* **294–301**, 294 (ill.)
Macdonald, Margaret
   B *2:* 297
Macdonald, Marion
   B *2:* 294
Macdonald, Ranald
   B *2:* 294
Madison, Dolly
   B *2:* 306–7, 310 (ill.)
Madison, James
   B *1:* 191, 225, 226, 242; *2:* 302
   (ill.), **302–11**, 316, 318, 319
Madness of King George, The
   PS 16–17, 61
Maid of the Oaks
   B *1:* 79, 80
Man of Reason
   B *2:* 357
Manhattan
   A 128, 140
Mansfield, William
   A 122
Marie-Antoinette (queen)
   B *2:* 269, 272, 285
Marquis of Rockingham
   PS 20 (ill.), 20, 49
Marshfield, Massachusetts
   B *2:* 395
Martin, James Kirby
   B *1:* 42
Martin, Joseph Plumb
   PS 214, **221–27**
Martin, Josiah
   B *2:* 299, 300
Maryland
   PS 165–66
Maryland Journal
   B *1:* 174
Mason, Anne Eilbeck
   B *2:* 313, 314
Mason, George
   B *2:* 308, 312 (ill.), **312–20**,
   316 (ill.)
Mason, Sarah Brent
   B *2:* 317
Masons
   B *2:* 393
Massachusetts
   PS 55, 171–82
Massachusetts Bay Colony
   B *2:* 345

Massachusetts Charitable
   Fire Society
   B *2:* 398
Massachusetts Charitable
   Mechanics Association
   B *2:* 397
Massachusetts Circular Letter
   PS 29–30, 31
Massachusetts Committee of
   Safety
   B *2:* 393
Massachusetts General Court
   B *1:* 200
Massachusetts Government Act
   PS 39, 46
Massachusetts House of
   Representatives
   B *2:* 393
Massachusetts Magazine
   B *2:* 339
Massachusetts Provincial
   Congress
   B *1:* 203
Massachusetts State Convention
   B *1:* 207
Massachusetts State House
   B *2:* 397
McCauley, John
   B *2:* 324
McCauley, Mary ("Molly Pitcher")
   A 110
   B *2:* **321–27**, 321 (ill.), 324 (ill.)
McCrea, James
   B *2:* 328
McCrea, Jane
   A 117–18, 161
   B *2:* 328 (ill.), **328–37**, 331 (ill.)
McCrea, John
   B *2:* 328, 333
McDonald, Donald
   B *2:* 299
McKean, Thomas
   PS 131
McNeil, Sara
   B *2:* 329
Medfield, Massachusetts
   B *2:* 340
Medical care
   A 152
Medium, or A Happy Tea-Party, The
   B *2:* 343
Memoirs (Horace Walpole)
   B *2:* 459

Memoirs of the Last Ten Years of the Reign of George II
B *2:* 465
Memoirs of the Reign of King George III
B *2:* 465
Mercer, John
B *2:* 312
Meyer, Edith Patterson
B *1:* 211, 215
Mifflin, Thomas
B *2:* 429
Miles, Wesley
B *2:* 325
Military Academy. *See* U.S. Military Academy
Militia
A 95, 99, 186
Miller, John C.
B *1:* 108
Millstone, New Jersey
B *1:* 110
Minute Men
B *2:* 444
Mobile, Alabama
B *1:* 151
Modlin, Joseph
B *2:* 350
Mohawk
A 118–19
B *1:* 54, 55, 57, 59–61, 63–65, 67–69
Moland, John
B *1:* 106
Monmouth, Battle of
B *2:* 323, 324, 326
Monmouth, New Jersey
B *2:* 321, 323, 326, 327
Monroe, James
B *2:* 358
PS 99
Montclair, Marquis de
B *1:* 98
Monticello
B *1:* 246, 247, 255
Montpelier estate
B *2:* 311
Montreal, Quebec, Canada
B *1:* 34, 40
Moore's Creek Bridge, North Carolina
B *2:* 299, 300

Morris, Robert
B *1:* 110; *2:* 279, 418, 420 (ill.)
PS 249
Morris, William
B *1:* 196
Morristown, New Jersey
A 151–52, 157, 176
B *1:* 110
Morse, Jedidiah
B *2:* 341
Moses Kill, New York
B *2:* 333
Mount Olivet Cemetery
B *2:* 280
Mount Vernon, Virginia
A 183
B *2:* 479, 481 (ill.), 488
Mum Bett. *See* Freeman, Elizabeth
Mumbet. *See* Freeman, Elizabeth
Munich, Germany
B *1:* 103
Murray, John (clergyman)
B *2:* 339, 343
Murray, John (politician). *See* Dunmore, Lord
Murray, Judith Sargent
B *2:* 338 (ill.), **338–44**

N

Nagle, Patrick
B *1:* 81
Narrative of Colonel Ethan Allen's Captivity
B *1:* 35
Narrative of Some of the Adventures, Dangers, and Sufferings of a Revolutionary Soldier, A
PS 214, **221–27**
Natchez, Mississippi
B *2:* 338
National Archives
PS 148
National Assembly
B *2:* 287, 291
National Republican Party
B *1:* 17
Native Americans. *See also* Indians
A 3, 41, 43, 95, 107, 115–16, 161, 187
B *1:* 54–61, 63–69, 118, 151,

152, 164–71; *2:* 330, 331, 334, 335
  PS 3, 164, 165 (ill.)
Naval Academy. *See* U.S. Naval Academy
Navigation Acts
  A 3, 45
Navy. *See* U.S. Navy
Nevis, British West Indies
  B *1:* 187
New Hampshire Grants
  B *1:* 32
New Haven, Connecticut
  B *1:* 39
New Jersey campaign
  A 142, 144, 146, 148, 158
New Jersey Medical Society
  B *2:* 346
New Jersey Plan
  B *2:* 305
New Jersey Provincial Congress
  B *2:* 347
New London, Connecticut
  B *1:* 43
New Orleans, Louisiana
  B *1:* 150, 151
New Providence, Nassau, Bahamas
  B *1:* 153
New Rochelle, New York
  B *2:* 357
New Spain
  B *1:* 148
New York Assembly
  PS 26
New York campaign
  A 127, 129, 131, 136, 138, 139 (ill.), 140–42, 145
New York City Common Council
  B *1:* 196
New-York Gazetteer
  B *2:* 408, 410, 411
New York, New York
  A 105–6, 127–29, 171, 181, 185
  B *1:* 34, 99, 102, 180, 187, 188, 190, 195, 232; *2:* 277, 347, 350, 359, 394, 405, 413, 415, 486
Newark, New Jersey
  B *2:* 340, 345
Newberry, John
  A 30

Newport, Rhode Island
  A 177
  B *1:* 206; *2:* 396
Newspapers in Colonial America
  B *1:* 174; *2:* 408, 410–15
Noailles, Adrienne de
  B *2:* 265
Nonimportation policies
  A 48
North, Sir Frederick
  A 64, 67, 74, 78
  B *1:* 159, 161
  PS 38–39, 47, 48, 51, 127
Norwich, Connecticut
  B *1:* 38

O

"Objections to the Proposed Federal Constitution"
  B *2:* 318
Odell, Jonathan
  B *2:* **345–52**
Odell, Mary
  B *2:* 347
Odell, William Franklin
  B *2:* 347, 352
Ohio Company
  B *2:* 313, 314
Old Granary Burying Ground
  B *1:* 29
Old Mill Prison
  B *2:* 422
Old North Church
  B *2:* 395
Olive Branch Petition
  A 87, 93
  B *1:* 35, 109
  PS 57, **127–33**
Oliver, Andrew
  PS 170, 191, 193, 194, 195, 197, 200
Ollive, Elizabeth
  B *2:* 355
On American Taxation
  B *1:* 84
"On Conciliation"
  PS **49–54**
On the Equality of the Sexes
  B *2:* 340
Oneida
  A 116, 119

Onion River Land Company
B *1:* 32, 35
Otis, James
A 31
B *1:* 188; *2:* 393

P

Pain, Frances Cocke
B *2:* 353
Pain, Joseph
B *2:* 353
Paine, Thomas
A 35, 102–3, 149
B *1:* 87, 88; *2:* 351, 353 (ill.),
353–60, 358 (ill.), 428
PS 61, **97–106**, 214, **229–34**
Palace of Versailles
B *2:* 266, 269, 275
Panther
B *2:* 331
Paris, France
B *1:* 250; *2:* 265, 270, 275, 427
Parish, Elijah
B *2:* 341
Parks Commission of
Washington, D.C.
B *2:* 280
Parliament
A 46–47, 54, 57, 63, 67, 73, 77,
102, 184
B *1:* 74, 76, 106, 118, 120, 156,
200; *2:* 366
Parliamentary monarchy
B *2:* 270
Paterson, New Jersey
B *2:* 279
Paterson, William
B *1:* 110
Paul Revere's Ride
B *2:* 391, 395
Peacock Tavern
B *1:* 29
Peale, Charles Willson
A 38
Pendleton, Edmund
B *2:* 316
Penn, Richard
PS 130
Penn, William
PS 130
Pennsylvania Assembly
B *1:* 106, 108, 111

Pennsylvania Gazette
A 33
B *1:* 116, 117, 123
PS 79
Pennsylvania General Assembly
B *2:* 357
Pennsylvania Historical Society
B *2:* 418
Pennsylvania Hospital
B *2:* 429
Pennsylvania Magazine
B *2:* 355
Pennsylvania Society for
Promoting the Abolition of
Slavery
B *2:* 431
Penobscot Expedition
B *2:* 396
Penobscot, Maine
B *2:* 396
Pensacola, Florida
B *1:* 151
Philadelphia, Pennsylvania
A 131, 148, 158, 164, 168
B *1:* 12, 28, 35, 40, 93, 106,
108, 112, 130, 188, 190,
203, 204, 220, 223, 233;
2: 259, 276, 303, 305, 312,
316, 339, 347, 348, 355,
394, 417–19, 421, 422, 424,
428, 430, 432, 483
Phillipe, Louis
B *2:* 272
*Philosophical Enquiry into the
Origin of Our Ideas of the
Sublime and Beautiful, A*
B *1:* 82
Phyfe, Duncan
B *2:* 277
Pilgrims
A 2
Pinckney, Thomas
B *1:* 194
Pitcher, Molly. *See* McCauley,
Mary ("Molly Pitcher")
Pitt, William
A 49, 101
B *2:* 361 (ill.), **361–69**, 457, 501
PS 22–23
Pitt, William, the Younger
B *1:* 162
Plymouth Colony
PS 1

Plymouth, England
B *2:* 422
Poems on Various Subjects, Religious and Moral
B *2:* 493
Poetry
A 153
Poles in the American Revolution
B *2:* 259
Polk, James K.
B *2:* 384
Pontiac
A 42, 42 (ill.)
B *1:* 55
Pontiac's Rebellion
A 42–43
Poor Richard's Almanack
A 30
B *1:* 123
Poor, Salem
B *1:* 46, **51–52**
PS 79
Population statistics
A 175
Postal Service. *See* U.S. Postal Service
Potomac River
B *2:* 279
Prescott, William
A 86, 88
Preston, Thomas
A 59–60
PS 35–36
Primrose, Lady
B *2:* 298
Princess Amelia. *See* Amelia (princess)
Princess Augusta. *See* Augusta (princess)
Princeton, New Jersey
A 136, 150
B *1:* 189, 232; *2:* 427
Princeton University
B *2:* 302, 345, 426
Privateers
B *2:* 376
Privy Council
PS 196, 197, 198, 200
Proclamation of Rebellion
A 90
PS 55–62
Proclamation of 1763
A 44–45

Prospect, The
B *2:* 354
Providence Gazette
B *1:* 174, 175
Pulaski, Casimir
B *2:* **370–78**, 370 (ill.), 376 (ill.)
Puritans
B *1:* 115
Putnam, Israel
A 86, 95

Q

Quakers
B *1:* 105; *2:* 419, 422, 424
Quartering Act
A 47, 58
B *1:* 142
PS 26, 39–40, 45–46, 65
Quebec, Canada
B *1:* 39, 98
PS 117, 203
Queen Anne. *See* Anne (queen)
Queen Charlotte Sophia. *See* Charlotte Sophia (queen)
Queen Elizabeth II. *See* Elizabeth II (queen)
Queen Marie-Antoinette. *See* Marie-Antoinette (queen)
Querno, Camillo
B *2:* 351
Quincy, Josiah
B *1:* 24
Quincy, Massachusetts
B *1:* 9, 18, 198

R

Rall, Johann Gottlieb
A 147, 150
Ramsay, David
B *2:* 379 (ill.), **379–84**
Randall, William Sterne
B *1:* 255
Randolph, Jane
B *1:* 246
Randolph, Peyton
A 75
B *1:* 205
PS 108 (ill.), 108, 114–15
Randolph, Virginia
PS 137

Rangers
   B *1:* 181; *2:* 437
Rawdon-Hastings, Francis
   A 138
Reason, the Only Oracle of Man
   B *1:* 36
*Records of the Life of the Rev. John
    Murray, Written by Him*
   B *2:* 343
Red Jacket
   B *1:* 57, 58
Redcoats
   A 58, 129, 136–37, 140, 142,
    144–45, 159–60, 162, 174,
    181, 183–84, 186
Redmond, John
   B *2:* 426
Reed, Esther De Berdt
   B *2:* **385–90,** 385 (ill.)
Reed, Joseph
   B *2:* 385, 386
*Reflections on the Revolution in
    France and on the Proceedings
    of Certain Societies in London*
   B *1:* 87
Religion
   B *2:* 308
Religious freedom
   A 1
Religious persecution
   B *2:* 505
Religious Society of Friends
   B *2:* 417
"Report on the Public Credit"
   B *1:* 192
Republican Party
   B *1:* 17, 18, 226; *2:* 307, 310
Resolves of the House of
    Representatives . . .
   PS **191–96**
Restraining Acts
   A 67
   PS 26
Revere Copper and Brass
    Company
   B *2:* 397
Revere, Paul
   A 60, 80, 80 (ill.)
   B *1:* 144, 204; *2:* 391 (ill.),
    391–98, 396 (ill.), 441
   PS 213
Revere, Rachel Walker
   B *2:* 398

Rhode Island
   PS 16
Rhode Island Regiment
   A 120
Rice
   PS 116
Richmond, Virginia
   A 181
   B *1:* 43, 93, 220, 225, 250
Riedesel, Frederika von
   A 162
   B *2:* **399–407**
Riedesel, Friederich Adolphus von
   B *2:* 400–405
Rights of Man, The
   B *1:* 87; *2:* 357
   PS 99
Riots
   A 48, 48 (ill.)
Rivington, James
   B *2:* 348, **408–16,** 408 (ill.)
Roanoke, Virginia
   PS 1
Robespierre, Maximilien de
   B *2:* 359
Rochambeau, Jean Baptiste
   A 177, 181–83, 183 (ill.)
Rockingham, Charles Watson
   B *1:* 158
Rodney, Caesar
   A 76
Rogers, Loula Kendall
   B *1:* 212
Rome, Italy
   B *2:* 279
Ross, Betsy
   B *2:* 417 (ill.), **417–25,** 420 (ill.)
Ross, George
   B *2:* 418, 420 (ill.)
Ross, John
   B *2:* 418
Ross, Lucilla
   B *2:* 422
*Rules by Which a Great Empire May
    Be Reduced to a Small One*
   PS 78–79
Rush, Benjamin
   B *1:* 194; *2:* 355, 359, 379, 382,
    426–33, 427 (ill.)
Rush, Julia Stockton
   B *2:* 427
Rush Medical College
   B *2:* 432

Rush, Richard
  B *2:* 427
Rutledge, Edward
  PS 152

S

Saar, Doreen Alvarez
  B *1:* 101
St. Johns, New Brunswick,
    Canada
  B *1:* 33, 39, 44
St. Paul's Chapel
  B *2:* 277
Salem, Massachusetts
  B *1:* 143; *2:* 395
Salisbury, England
  B *1:* 98
Sampson, Deborah
  B *2:* 434 (ill.), **434–42,** 437 (ill.)
Saratoga campaign
  B *1:* 78, 79
Saratoga, New York
  A 161–62, 162 (ill.), 167
  B *1:* 40, 233; *2:* 260, 402,
    414, 444
Sarcelles, France
  B *1:* 97
Sargent, Winthrop
  B *2:* 338, 348
Savannah, Georgia
  A 173, 176
  B *1:* 93; *2:* 276, 377
Scalping
  B *1:* 167; *2:* 330, 334
Schuyler, Philip
  A 94, 127, 129–30, 130 (ill.),
    160
  B *1:* 34, 110, 189; *2:* 403
Seabury, Samuel
  B *2:* 348
Sears, Isaac
  B *2:* 412, 415
Second Continental Congress. *See
    also* Continental Congress;
    First Continental Congress
  A 84, 89, 93–94
  B *1:* 13, 28, 120, 198, 204, 223,
    240, 248, 249; *2:* 303, 418,
    482, 483
  PS 43, 109–11, **127–33,**
    135–49, 151–68

Secretary of Defense
  B *1:* 15
Sedgwick, Theodore, Sr.
  B *1:* 132–34
Seven Years' War
  A 41
  B *1:* 72, 73; *2:* 364
Shadwell, Virginia
  B *1:* 246
Shays, Daniel
  B *1:* 207; *2:* 443 (ill.), **443–50**
Shays's Rebellion
  B *1:* 135, 207; *2:* 443, 446,
    447, 449
Sheffield Declaration
  B *1:* 132
Shepard, William
  B *2:* 448
Sherman, Roger
  A 76, 132
  B *1:* 14
  PS 135–36
Shippen, William
  B *2:* 428
*Short History of the American
    Revolution, A*
  B *1:* 33; *2:* 356
Six Nations Iroquois Confederacy
  A 115, 118
*Sketches of Eighteenth Century
    America, or More Letters from
    an American Farmer*
  B *1:* 102
Skye, Scotland
  B *2:* 298
Slavery
  A 100–101, 107, 120, 122, 124,
    124 (ill.), 135, 172, 177
  B *1:* 46–48, 50, 51, 131, 133,
    134, 136, 241, 249; *2:* 261,
    262, 318, 381, 382, 431, 489,
    491, 494
  PS 87, 114–16, 218,
    219–20, 235
Smallpox
  A 43, 47, 103, 110, 151–52
  B *1:* 117
Smith, Abigail. *See* Adams, Abigail
Smuggling
  A 45–46
  B *1:* 200
Social classes
  A 7, 10

Society of Free Quakers
  B *2:* 422
Society of Friends
  B *1:* 105; *2:* 353
  PS 69, 105
Society of the Cincinnati
  B *2:* 260, 277, 280
Somersett, James
  A 122
Sons of Liberty
  A 49–51, 121
  B *2:* 393, 394, 411–13,
    470, 504
  PS 4, 15–16, 33, 34, 172, 178,
    179, 186
South Carolina
  PS 116
South Uist, Hebrides
  B *2:* 294
Southern campaign
  A 172–73, 176–77
Southern colonies
  A 172, 177
Spies in the American Revolution
  A 93, 141, 143
  B *1:* 178–83, 185, 212; *2:* 415
Spotswood, Alexander
  PS 93
Stamp Act
  A 20, 45, 45 (ill.), 47–48, 50,
    57, 70
  B *1:* 11, 23, 74, 75, 106, 119,
    158, 199, 200, 219; *2:* 314,
    365, 368, 411, 456, 461, 469
  PS 4, **7–18**, 9 (ill.), 14 (ill.), 23,
    131, 148, 180 (ill.)
Stamp Act Congress
  B *1:* 107
  PS 15
Stamp Act Resolves
  B *1:* 219
Stansbury, Joseph
  B *2:* 348
Steel, Tom
  B *2:* 299
Steuben, Frederick von
  B *2:* 276
Steuben, Friedrich Wilhelm
    Augustus von
  B *2:* 483
Stevens, John
  B *2:* 338
Stockbridge Indians
  A 115

Stokesbury, James L.
  B *1:* 33; *2:* 356
Stony Point, New York
  B *2:* 445
Story of Margaretta, The
  B *2:* 342, 343
Strahan, William
  PS 35, 78 (ill.), 79–80
Stratford, Virginia
  B *1:* 224
Stuart, Charles Edward
  B *2:* 294–96, 297 (ill.), 298, 301
Stuart, Gilbert
  A 38, 38 (ill.)
Stuart, John, Earl of Bute
  B *1:* 155
Sugar Act
  A 46
  B *2:* 314, 365
Sullivan, James
  B *1:* 208
Summary History of New England, A
  B *2:* 340
*Summary View of the Rights of
    British America, A*
  A 61
  B *1:* 247
  PS **81–88**, 137
Supply shortages
  A 160, 178
Supreme Court. *See* U.S.
    Supreme Court
Swallow
  B *2:* 419

T

Taft, William Howard
  B *2:* 280
Talbot County, Maryland
  B *1:* 105
Tallmadge, Benjamin
  B *1:* 179
Tarring and feathering
  PS 30 (ill.), 30, 123
Tax acts
  PS 7–18, 19–23, 25–36, 37–48,
    171–82, 183–89, 191–96
Taxation by U.S. government
  B *2:* 443, 447
Taxation of American colonies
  B *1:* 22–24, 84, 86, 105–7, 157,
    159, 160, 188, 199, 219; *2:*

302, 314, 356, 361, 364, 366–68, 394, 411, 428, 456, 465, 482

"Taxation without representation"
A 47, 49, 54, 62, 64–65

Taylor, Moses Coit
B 2: 350

Tea Act
A 52, 64
B 1: 26; 2: 428, 470
PS 37, 179

Temple, John
PS 197

Thacher, James
A 169, 183

Thomas Paine National Historical Association
PS 105

Thomson, Charles
PS 146

Thoughts on the Cause of the Present Discontents
B 1: 84

Ticonderoga, New York
B 2: 259, 401, 438

Ticonderoga, New York, Battle of
B 2: 259

Tobacco
A 2

Toledo, Ohio
B 2: 487

Tories
B 1: 13, 211, 216

Townshend Acts
A 51, 54, 62
B 1: 75, 107, 159; 2: 314, 367, 393, 457, 470
PS 63–64, 148, 172, 174

Townshend, Charles
A 51, 51 (ill.)
B 1: 158; 2: **451–58**, 451 (ill.)
PS 25, 26, 27, 35

Townshend Revenue Act
PS **25–36**

Traveller Returned, The
B 2: 343

Treaty of Ghent
B 2: 310

Treaty of Paris
A 119, 185, 186 (ill.)
B 1: 15, 29, 153, 161, 242, 244; 2: 314, 317, 485
PS 123, 233, 249

Trenton, New Jersey
A 136, 142, 148
B 1: 189, 232; 2: 375, 414

Trinity College
B 1: 81

Trudeau, Garry
PS 105

Trumbull, John
A 34

Tuscarora
A 119

U

U.S. Constitution
A 118
B 1: 112, 191, 207, 226, 242; 2: 302, 303, 305, 311, 312, 397
PS 148, 251

U.S. Department of the Treasury
B 1: 192

U.S. Military Academy
B 2: 281

U.S. Naval Academy
B 1: 192

U.S. Navy
B 1: 192

U.S. Postal Service
B 1: 174

U.S. Supreme Court
B 1: 243; 2: 280

U.S.S. Constitution
B 2: 397

Universal History Americanized
B 2: 384

Universalist
B 2: 339

Universalist Quarterly
B 2: 339

University of Edinburgh
B 2: 426

University of Pennsylvania
B 1: 118

University of Vermont
B 1: 35

University of Virginia
B 1: 255; 2: 311

V

Valerius
B 1: 111

Valley Forge, Pennsylvania
  A 116, 167 (ill.), 168, 168 (ill.)
  B 1: 35, 232; 2: 266, 276, 327,
    421, 483
Van Doren, Carl
  B 1: 40
Vanderlyn, John
  B 2: 335
Vermont, Republic of
  B 1: 35
Versailles, France
  B 2: 265, 279
View of Religions, A
  B 2: 340
Vindication of Natural Society, A
  B 1: 82
Vining, Elizabeth Gray
  B 2: 296, 298
Virginia
  A 179
Virginia Convention
  B 1: 223; 2: 314
Virginia Council of State
  B 2: 304
Virginia Declaration of Rights
  B 2: 303, 308, 316, 319
Virginia delegates
  PS 114–15
Virginia House of Burgesses
  B 1: 219, 220, 224, 247; 2: 313
  PS 81, 89, 108
Virginia, martial law in
  PS 217–20
Virginia militia
  B 1: 13
Virginia Plan
  B 2: 305
Virginia Statute for Religious
    Freedom
  B 1: 249
Voting rights
  B 2: 447, 448

W

Wallace, Mike
  PS 105
Walpole, Horace
  B 2: 454, 459 (ill.), 459–67
  PS 215, 241–45, 242 (ill.)
Walpole, Robert
  B 2: 459

War of 1812
  B 1: 17, 58; 2: 281, 309,
    310, 424
Ward, Artemas
  A 94
Ward, Samuel
  PS 16
Warner, Seth
  B 1: 34
Warren, Joseph
  B 2: 393
Warren, Mercy Otis
  B 2: 333, 343, 393, 468 (ill.),
    468–77, 472 (ill.)
Washington, D.C.
  B 1: 41, 253; 2: 275, 281,
    282, 310
Washington, George
  A 75, 87, 87 (ill.), 89, 93–96,
    99, 103–4, 106–7, 129–30,
    137, 139–44, 145 (ill.), 146,
    147 (ill.), 148, 152, 157–58,
    163, 166–67, 171, 176, 179,
    179 (ill.), 181, 183, 185
  B 1: 13–15, 26, 28, 29, 33, 35,
    40, 42, 43, 52, 67, 101, 110,
    111, 140, 187, 189, 192, 193,
    206, 226, 231, 233, 243;
    2: 260, 264–66, 273, 276,
    277, 278 (ill.), 281, 282, 306,
    313, 315, 317, 319, 323, 324,
    326, 327, 332, 343, 351, 356,
    374, 375, 403, 408, 413, 415,
    418–20, 420 (ill.), 424, 428,
    430, 478 (ill.), 478–88
  PS 12–13, 93, 98, 99, 101, 104,
    115, 128–29, 139, 204, 205,
    206, 207, 214, 215, 226–27,
    229–32, 230 (ill.), 238,
    247–53, 249 (ill.)
Washington, Martha Dandridge
    Custis
  B 2: 481
Waterloo, Belgium
  B 2: 272
  PS 12
Watson-Wentworth, Charles
  PS 20 (ill.), 20, 49
Wayne, Anthony, General
  B 2: 445
Weaponry
  A 109, 111
Webster, Daniel
  B 2: 311

Webster, John
  B *2:* 417
Webster, Noah
  A 29
Wedding, colonial
  A 25 (ill.)
Weehawken, New Jersey
  B *1:* 195
Weisgerber, C. H.
  B *2:* 424
Wentworth, Charles Watson,
    Second Marquis of
    Rockingham
  B *1:* 83, 87
West, Benjamin
  A 38
West Point, New York
  B *1:* 43; *2:* 260, 281, 436, 439
Westchester, New York
  B *1:* 99
Wetherill, Samuel
  B *2:* 419
Whately, Thomas
  PS 171, 172, 187, 193, 197, 198
Wheatley, Phillis
  B *1:* 206; *2:* **489–98**, 490 (ill.)
Wheeling, West Virginia
  B *1:* 215
Whig Party (England)
  B *1:* 17, 156
Whiskey Rebellion
  B *1:* 193; *2:* 488
White House
  B *1:* 16; *2:* 310
White Plains, New York
  B *1:* 189, 232
Whiting, John
  PS 204, 205–6
Wilkes Booth, John
  B *2:* 504
Wilkes, John
  B *2:* **499–506**, 499 (ill.)
Wilkinson, Eliza
  PS 214, **235–39**
Williamsburg, Virginia
  B *1:* 222, 246; *2:* 304
Willison, George F.
  B *1:* 221
Wilmington, Delaware
  B *1:* 112
Wilmington, North Carolina
  B *1:* 105
Wilson, David
  B *2:* 330

Wolf, James
  B *1:* 156
Women and the Revolutionary
    War
  A 76 (ill.), 110, 134
  B *1:* 93, 211, 215; *2:* 294, 321,
    322, 326, 336, 340, 402, 417
Women Invited to War
  B *2:* 340
Women's rights
  A 135
  B *1:* 176; *2:* 336, 338, 339, 341,
    342, 423, 431
Worcester, Massachusetts
  B *2:* 396
Wordsworth, William
  B *1:* 89
Wright, James
  PS 108
Writs of assistance
  PS 27–28
Wyoming Valley (Pennsylvania)
    Massacre
  A 118

X

XYZ Affair
  B *1:* 16

Y

"Yankee"
  PS 226
"Yankee Doodle"
  B *1:* 210
  PS 226
"Yankee ingenuity"
  A 141
Yankees
  A 109
Yellow fever
  B *2:* 423, 430
Yorktown, Battle of
  B *1:* 161
Yorktown campaign
  B *1:* 190
Yorktown, New York
  B *1:* 36
Yorktown, Pennsylvania
  B *1:* 190; *2:* 422
Yorktown, Virginia